Enduro Racing

by Steve Hendrickson

Consultant:
Hugh Fleming
Director, AMA Sports
American Motorcyclist Association

CAPSTONE BOOKS

an imprint of Capstone Press
Mankato, Minnesota

Capstone Books are published by Capstone Press
151 Good Counsel Drive, P.O. Box 669, Mankato, Minnesota 56002
http://www.capstone-press.com

Library of Congress Cataloging-in-Publication Data
Hendrickson, Steve.
  Enduro racing/by Steve Hendrickson.
  p. cm.—(Motorcycles)
  Includes bibliographical references (p. 44) and index.
  Summary: An introduction to the history, development, equipment, and stars of
the sport of enduro racing.
  ISBN 0-7368-0477-3
  1. Motocross—Juvenile literature. [1. Motocross. 2. Motorcycle racing.] I. Title.
II. Series.

GV1060.12. H45 2000
796.7'56—dc21   99-052612

Editorial Credits
Blake Hoena, editor; Timothy Halldin, cover designer and illustrator; Heidi Schoof and
    Jodi Theisen, photo researchers

Photo Credits
Mark Kariya, cover, 4, 7, 9, 10, 12, 15, 16, 18, 21, 22, 24, 26, 29, 31, 34, 37, 38, 41, 45

1 2 3 4 5 6 05 04 03 02 01 00

Table of Contents

CHAPTER 1

Enduro Racing

Motorcycle enduros are races of skill and timing. The fastest racers do not always win enduro races. Instead, it is the most accurate racers who succeed. Each enduro race has an exact time in which racers try to complete the race. Racers who complete a course too fast or too slow do not win.

A motorcycle enduro tests racers' skills. Racers must ride safely over all kinds of terrain. Enduro courses can run through woods, valleys, and swamps. Racers even may have to ride over rocks and hills. But timing is important in enduro racing. Successful enduro racers must be able to keep track of their speed, distance traveled, and time while riding over rough terrain.

Enduro racers ride over rough terrain.

Checkpoints

Checkpoints are located along enduro courses. Racers must stop and check in with race officials at checkpoints. These officials check the time racers arrive at checkpoints.

Each racer is supposed to check in at a certain time. Racers who check in on time receive no points. Racers who check in early or late receive penalty points. The racer with the fewest penalty points at the end of the race wins.

Enduro Courses

Most enduro courses are narrow dirt paths wide enough for only one motorcycle. Enduro officials generally do not use roads when laying out courses. Enduro courses are marked with signs.

A typical enduro course is between 40 to 80 miles (64 to 129 kilometers) long. An enduro may take racers four to eight hours to complete. This time depends on a racer's skills and the length of the course.

Enduro courses usually are wide enough for only one motorcycle.

Federation of International Motorcyclists

The Federation of International Motorcyclists (FIM) is a group of motorcycle organizations from different countries. It helps organize and set rules for international enduro races. Racers from several countries participate in these races.

The first enduro was held in England in 1904. At the time, this type of race was called a cross-country race. The International Federation of Motorcycle Clubs set the rules for this race. Later, this organization became the FIM.

In 1913, the FIM sponsored the first International Six Days Enduro (ISDE). This race was held in England. The ISDE is one of the best known enduro races. Since 1913, the ISDE has been held in a different country each year. The 1999 ISDE took place in Portugal.

American Motorcyclist Association

The American Motorcyclist Association (AMA) first organized motorcycle racing

Racers need dependable motorcycles to succeed at enduro racing.

**The American Motorcyclist Association
sanctions most North American races.**

events in 1924. The AMA sanctions most
North American motorcycle races. Sanctioned
races are official AMA racing events. These
races follow AMA rules and guidelines.

Motorcycle clubs sponsor enduro races.
Club officials choose the location and the
route for enduros. Club officials must follow
AMA and FIM rules as they lay out enduro
courses. On long courses, gasoline must be
available for racers. This can be at a gas station

or a place where racers can leave a gas can. Some enduros include a sidecar class. This small car is attached to the side of a motorcycle for carrying passengers. Club officials then must make sure the course is wide enough for sidecars.

The AMA sanctions both amateur and professional races. Amateur racers compete for fun and personal challenge. They do not race for money. Professional racers can earn money for racing.

The AMA works to improve motorcycle racing and motorcyclists' rights. It sanctions local and national races. The AMA also works with national governments to support laws that protect motorcyclists' rights. The AMA has more than 240,000 members. It publishes its own magazine called *American Motorcyclist*.

CHAPTER 2

Enduro Basics

Enduro racing is difficult. Racers must keep track of their speed while riding over rough terrain. They also need to know the distance between checkpoints and the time it takes to reach each checkpoint.

Timing and Distance
The time an enduro starts is called the key time. Before the key time, race organizers give racers a route sheet. The route sheet lists the exact distances between checkpoints. It lists the times racers should arrive at each checkpoint. The route sheet also lists the average speed racers should travel between checkpoints.

Racers need to keep track of their time and speed while racing over rough terrain.

Racers must keep track of the route sheet information during a race. Many racers use roll charts. They write important information about the enduro course on these long strips of paper. This information may include the distance between checkpoints and the time it takes to reach each checkpoint. Racers attach roll charts to the handlebars of their motorcycles. This helps them keep track of their time and speed during races.

Running the Enduro

An enduro might include as many as 100 motorcycle racers. But these racers cannot all start at once. Courses usually are too narrow. Race officials assign each racer a number. They then allow up to four racers to leave the starting line every minute.

Signs along the course tell racers where to turn. These signs let racers know if they are going the right way. Other signs may point out dangers near the course. Signs also may let racers know if they have made a wrong turn. Racers who correctly follow the signs will reach the checkpoints.

Race officials only allow up to four racers to start at one time.

Reaching Checkpoints

Before each checkpoint, racers must watch their motorcycle's odometer. This instrument shows racers how far they have traveled. They also need to check the time and compare that information to the route sheet. Racers then can tell if they will arrive at the checkpoint on time.

Officials note racers' times when they arrive at checkpoints. At most checkpoints, racers' times are recorded to the nearest minute. The

officials then add penalty points to racers' scores if they are too early or too late. Late racers need to make up time so they are not late at the next checkpoint.

Officials sometimes help racers by having "resets" at some checkpoints. A reset gives racers extra time to reach the next checkpoint. Racers who are on time can use this extra time to rest. Racers who are late can use the extra time to catch up by the next checkpoint.

After the race, checkpoint officials add up the penalty points that each racer earned. The racer with the fewest penalty points wins.

Types of Checkpoints

During the race, racers must stop at several types of checkpoints. AMA rules state that each of these checkpoints must be at least 3 miles (4.8 kilometers) apart.

Known controls are checkpoints that racers know about. Known controls are listed on route sheets. Officials record racers' times at these checkpoints. Yellow flags mark known controls.

Checkpoint officials write down racers' times.

Observation controls are checkpoints that racers do not know about. Officials do not record racers' times at observation controls. Officials at observation controls make sure that racers are staying on the course. White flags mark observation controls.

Secret controls are checkpoints that are not listed on the route sheet. Racers do not know about these controls. But racers' times are recorded at secret controls. Red and white flags mark secret controls.

Emergency controls are similar to secret controls. Racers do not know where these checkpoints are. But racers' times are recorded in minutes and seconds at emergency controls. Green and white flags mark emergency controls.

Gasoline stops and rest stops are located along enduro routes. Gas stops might be at gas stations or places where racers can leave their own gas can. Rest stops are called free time. They are marked on the route sheet. Racers are allowed to stop, rest, drink fluids, and eat at rest stops.

Yellow flags mark known controls.

Safety Rules

The AMA has safety rules for enduro races. Enduro races are not run on public roads. But races may cross streets. Racers must have a driver's license because of this. Racers must stop when an enduro course crosses a public road. Racers who break traffic laws are disqualified from the race.

Racers must respect the land enduro races are held on. Many environmentalists do not like off-road races such as enduros. These people care about nature. Many environmentalists think that enduro races harm wildlife. In some areas, racers need a spark arrestor on their motorcycle's muffler. This device prevents sparks from flying out of the muffler. Sparks could start forest fires.

Racing Classes

The AMA divides enduro racers into classes. Racers are divided into different classes according to their age, riding ability, and their motorcycle's engine.

Racers must obey traffic laws when a course crosses public roads.

A spark arrestor prevents sparks from flying out of a muffler.

The AMA has classes for motorcycles with two-stroke and four-stroke engines. Two-stroke engines produce power with each turn of the engine. Four-stroke engines produce power with every two turns of the engine.

Four-stroke engines are divided into three classes. These include motorcycles with up to

250 cubic centimeter (cc) engines, 400cc engines, and 500cc or larger engines. Motorcycles with larger engines often are more powerful and faster than motorcycles with smaller engines.

Two-stroke engines may be divided into as many as six classes. These can range from minicycles to 250cc motorcycles. An enduro race may also include an open class. For this class, racers can use a motorcycle with any size engine.

Racers can race individually or as a member of a country's racing team. Racers must be a citizen of the country to race for one of its teams. Countries may have world trophy and junior teams. World trophy teams have six racers. Junior teams can have four racers. But racers must be under 24 years of age to race for a junior team.

CHAPTER 3

Equipment

Enduro racers need dependable motorcycles in order to succeed. But enduro racers also need other equipment to keep track of their time and distance traveled.

Helpful Equipment

Enduro racers often use basic equipment to keep track of their time and mileage. Racers can tell how far they have traveled by checking their motorcycle's odometer. Racers can keep track of time by using a wristwatch.

Some racers use small computers to keep track of their speed and distance traveled. Racers can attach these computers to their motorcycle's handlebars. The computers keep track of racers' time and mileage. The

Some racers use a wristwatch to keep track of their time.

Dirt bikes are the best bikes for enduro racing.

computers also let racers know if they are going too fast or too slow during a race.

Some racers use global positioning systems (GPS). A GPS computer sends signals to satellites. These spacecraft orbit Earth. A GPS can tell racers their exact location anywhere on Earth.

Dirt Bike Engines

Dirt bikes usually are the best motorcycles for enduro racing. These motorcycles are built for off-road use.

Two types of engines are used for dirt bikes. These are two-stroke and four-stroke engines. Each engine type has some advantages and disadvantages.

Since the 1960s, most dirt bikes have had two-stroke engines. Two-stroke engines are lightweight and contain fewer parts than four-stroke engines. They also can produce a great deal of power for their size. But two-stroke engines also create a great deal of pollution. Many two-stroke engines do not meet air pollution laws. Because of this, more dirt-bike manufacturers produce motorcycles with four-stroke engines.

Two-Stroke Engines

Two-stroke engines mix gas and oil together. This mixture is used both to supply power to the engine and to lubricate it. Lubrication keeps engine parts from rubbing against each other. Oil is used to lubricate engines.

Two-stroke engines have advantages and disadvantages. Two-stroke engines produce power with each turn of the engine. This allows them to produce more power than four-stroke engines. Two-stroke engines also have fewer parts and are lighter than four-stroke engines. But two-stroke engines use a mixture of oil and gasoline for fuel. Oil creates a great deal of pollution when burned. Oil also does not lubricate engines well when mixed with gasoline. Two-stroke engines wear out faster than four-stroke engines because of this.

Four-Stroke Engines

Four-stroke engines produce power with every two turns of the engine. Four-stroke engines do not mix oil and gasoline. Four-stroke engines produce less pollution because of this. Oil also lubricates engines better when not mixed with gasoline. Four-stroke engines often last longer than two-stroke engines.

Four-stroke engines also have some disadvantages. Four-stroke engines produce less power than two-stroke engines. Four-stroke

Four-stroke engines produce power with every other turn of the engine.

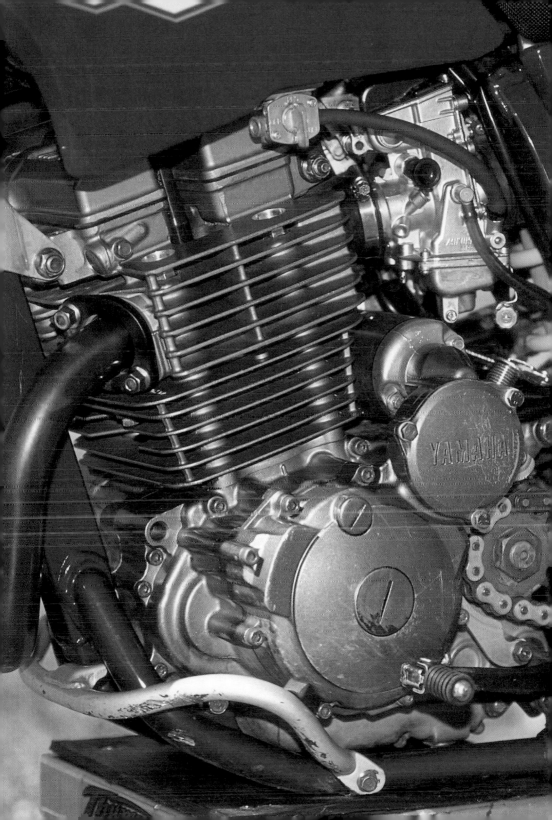

engines also need extra parts. Some of these parts control the fuel entering the engine and the exhaust exiting the engine. These extra parts make four-stroke engines heavier than two-stroke engines.

Suspension and Tires

Dirt bikes are good motorcycles to use for enduros. These motorcycles have a suspension system and tires designed for riding over rough terrain. The suspension system is the system of springs and shock absorbers on a motorcycle. This system absorbs the impact of riding over rough terrain.

A dirt bike's suspension system is designed to be ridden over bumps and rough terrain. On a dirt bike, the suspension has a great deal of travel. This is the distance a dirt bike's tire can move up or down. The travel on a dirt bike's suspension allows it to absorb the impact from being ridden over bumps and rocks. This makes the ride easier and smoother for racers.

Dirt bikes have knobby tires. The bumps on these tires allow them to grip dirt or muddy

The knobby tires on dirt bikes allow racers to ride on muddy trails.

trails. They also make it easier for enduro racers to ride their motorcycles over rocks and up hills.

Other Equipment

Dirt bikes have fenders. Their knobby tires throw mud, dirt, and small rocks in all directions. Fenders protect riders from these objects. But fenders must be far enough away from the tires. Mud and dirt may get packed between the fenders and tires. This can stop motorcycles.

Some enduro courses go through forests. The paths between trees can be very narrow. Enduro racers sometimes install narrow handlebars on their motorcycles. These handlebars make it easier to ride between trees. Racers also can install special handguards on the handlebars. Handguards protect racers' hands from trees and branches.

Some enduro motorcycles have extra-large gas tanks. This allows racers to ride farther without stopping for gas.

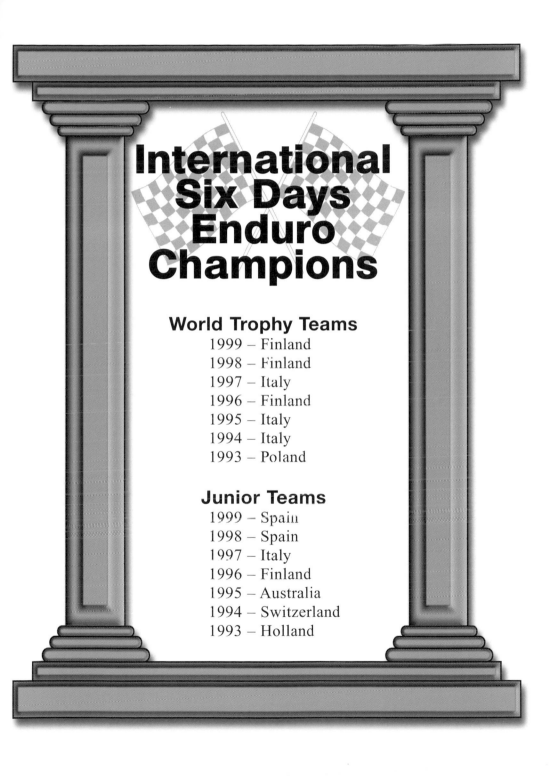

International Six Days Enduro Champions

World Trophy Teams

1999 – Finland
1998 – Finland
1997 – Italy
1996 – Finland
1995 – Italy
1994 – Italy
1993 – Poland

Junior Teams

1999 – Spain
1998 – Spain
1997 – Italy
1996 – Finland
1995 – Australia
1994 – Switzerland
1993 – Holland

CHAPTER 4

Skills and Safety

Beginning enduro racers often race beside more experienced racers. The experienced racers keep track of the time. This allows beginning racers to concentrate on the course. This also helps new racers learn how to keep track of time. They can watch how more experienced racers keep time. As racers gain experience, they then can start keeping time for themselves.

Preparing for a Race

Enduro races are physically difficult for racers. Racers often train to be in good physical condition. Most racers run or ride mountain bikes to stay in shape. It takes a great deal of

Enduro racing can be physically demanding.

energy to complete an enduro. Racers ride over rough terrain during enduros. Races also may last for several hours.

Racers often begin preparing the day before a race. Some racers eat foods with high levels of carbohydrates to give them energy. These foods include pasta dishes such as spaghetti and lasagna. Racers also avoid drinking caffeine or alcohol before a race. Caffeine and alcohol may cause dehydration. This condition is caused by lack of water in a person's body. Racers also need to get plenty of sleep before a race. Most enduros start early in the morning.

Safety During Races

Racers need special equipment to keep them safe. Helmets protect racers' heads during accidents. They wear heavy boots, gloves, and goggles for protection. Elbow pads, kneepads, shoulder pads, and chest protectors also protect racers if they crash.

It is also important for racers to eat and drink properly during an enduro. Dehydration

Racers prepare for a race by eating properly and studying the race's route sheet.

Racers must ride safely to protect themselves and other racers.

is one of the biggest dangers for racers during an enduro. Most racers carry water bottles. Racers also carry high-energy foods in case they get hungry or tired during a race. These foods contain a great deal of sugar and carbohydrates. Racers can leave food and drink at a gas stop. They then can pick up the food and water with their gas.

Motorcycles sometimes break down during an enduro. Many racers carry a small tool kit for quick repairs. Tool kits might include screwdrivers, wrenches, a small hammer, a knife, and a tire patch kit. Some racers also carry extra gloves and goggles in case their first set gets muddy.

Safe Riding

Enduro racing can be dangerous. Racers often race through woods and over unfamiliar terrain. Enduro racers must ride safely to protect themselves and other racers.

Racers must obey local and state traffic laws when they are on public land or roads. Racers also must stop before they cross a road that intersects the trail. Drivers of cars may not expect to see a motorcycle suddenly cross the road.

Most enduro trails are narrow. Slower racers should pull over to let faster racers pass them. Faster racers should be careful when passing slower racers to avoid accidents.

Racers sometimes crash and get injured. Racers who find an injured racer should stop to see if they can help. If they cannot help, they must report the injured racer at the next checkpoint. Race officials then can find and help any injured racers.

Racers should stay with their motorcycles if they break down. Racers also should stay near the trail. Racers who leave the trail might get lost or trespass on private property. It is easier for enduro officials to find and help racers if they stay near the trail.

Racers who do not finish enduros usually have mechanical problems during the race. Racers should make sure their motorcycles are safe and in good running condition. Their motorcycles should not have any loose or broken parts. The tires should be in good condition. Racers should also check the brakes and brake cables for wear.

Enduro racing can be an exciting and safe experience if racers follow safety rules. Racers then can enjoy the challenges of their sport.

Enduro racers need to make sure their motorcycles are in good running condition.

Words to Know

amateur (AM-uh-chur)—a racer who does not earn money for racing

dehydration (dee-HYE-dray-shuhn)—a health condition caused by lack of water

environmentalist (en-VYE-ruhn-men-tuhl-ist)—a person who is concerned about nature

fender (FEN-dur)—a covering over a motorcycle's wheel that protects the rider from flying mud and rocks

global positioning system (GLOH-buhl puh-ZI-shuh-ning SISS-tuhm)—an electronic tool used to find the location of a person or object anywhere on Earth

international race (in-tur-NASH-uh-nuhl RAYSS)—a race that includes racers from more than one country

lubricate (LOO-bruh-kate)—to add a substance such as oil to an engine; oil keeps engine parts from rubbing against each other.

muffler (MUHF-lur)—a device that reduces the noise made by an engine

odometer (oh-DAH-muh-tur)—an instrument that records how far a vehicle has been driven

professional (pruh-FESH-uh-nuhl)—a racer who can earn money racing

sanction (SANGK-shuhn)—to officially approve of a race; AMA-sanctioned races must follow AMA rules and guidelines.

suspension system (suh-SPEN-shuhn SISS-tuhm)—a system of springs and shock absorbers that absorbs the impact of riding over rough terrain

terrain (tuh-RAYN)—ground or land

travel (TRAV-uhl)—the distance a motorcycle's suspension system allows its tires to move up and down

To Learn More

Bales, Donnie and Gary Semics. *Pro Motocross and Off-Road Motorcycle Riding Techniques.* Osceola, Wis.: Motorbooks International, 1996.

Dregni, Michael. *Motorcycle Racing.* MotorSports. Mankato, Minn.: Capstone Books, 1994.

Jay, Jackson. *Motorcycles.* Rollin'. Mankato, Minn.: Capstone Books, 1996.

Otfinoski, Steven. *Wild on Wheels: Motorcycles Then and Now.* Here We Go! New York: Marshall Cavendish, 1998.

Useful Addresses

American Motorcyclist Association
13515 Yarmouth Drive
Pickerington, OH 43147

Canadian Motorcycle Association
P.O. Box 448
Hamilton, ON L8L 1J4
Canada

Federation of International Motorcyclists
11 Route Suisse
CH-1295 MIES
Switzerland

Internet Sites

All-OffRoad
http://www.all-offroad.com

American Motorcyclist Association
http://www.ama-cycle.org

Canadian Motorcycle Association
http://www.canmocycle.ca

East Coast Enduro Association
http://www.ecea.org

Federation of International Motorcyclists
http://www.fim.ch

Index